Movin

From Cubicle to Entrepreneurship
Volume 1

"Feed them w/ a long-handled spoon"
Karen's grandmother

Barbara here's to your dreams, passion, and to where God lead you.
Your Dreams... Your Passion... Your Life
Kar 2014

Karen M. Heck

COPYRIGHT

All rights reserved. No part of this publication may be reproduced or transmitted in any form or by any means, electronic or mechanical, including photocopying, recording, or by any informational storage or retrieval system, without the express written, dated, and signed permission of the author. Any unauthorized use, sharing, reproduction, or distribution is strictly prohibited.

Copyright © 2013 Karen M. Heck

All rights reserved.

ISBN10: 978-1492124962

ISBN-13:1492124966

CONTENTS

ACKNOWLEDGMENTS
DEDICATION
HOW TO USE THIS BOOK

DAY 1	1
DAY 2	4
DAY 3	7
DAY 4	10
DAY 5	13
DAY 6	16
DAY 7	18
DAY 8	20
DAY 9	22
DAY 10	24
DAY 11	26
DAY 12	29
DAY 13	31
DAY 14	33
DAY 15	35
DAY 16	38
DAY 17	41
DAY 18	43
DAY 19	46
DAY 20	49
DAY 21	51
DAY 22	54
DAY 23	56
DAY 24	59
DAY 25	62
DAY 26	64
DAY 27	67
DAY 28	69
DAY 29	71
DAY 30	74
DAY 31:	77

SUGGESTED RESOURCES
ABOUT THE AUTHOR

Acknowledgments

I want to thank all who have supported me in this journey of writing my first book!

My hubby, Richard Heck, for believing, supporting, and loving me through it all. I'm blessed that to have you as my hubby.

My mother, Joyce Washington who instilled in me good work ethics and encourages me to continue to move forward and not give up!

To my brothers, Tyrone and Damon Washington who always supports me in whatever it is I'm striving to accomplish and having my back.

My Virtual Assistant (VA), Melinda Ashley for all the hard work you put in helping me with my editing and getting this book in print.

Mary Dressen for being available, willing to read over what I had written and using her grammar expertise to help me pinpoint my language, grammar, and thoughts to make this readable.

My accountability partners in this world of entrepreneurship Dorea Walker and Bonnie Pond, who are also my friends. It's been my pleasure having you in my corner. I appreciate you being cheerleaders, encouragers, and for your ideas. Bonnie thank you for your guidance and help as I've walked through this journey of writing.

Gwen, my friend and the person who always believes in me and my entrepreneurial abilities even if when don't. Thank you for the long conversations, your constant and non-wavering support. You've always been there for the good, the bad, the ups and the down times. I'm grateful for your friendship!

Dedication

This book is for all those who are sitting at their desk wondering what am I doing here and dreaming about all they could be doing if they were not stuck in a cubical! It's dedicated to those who don't know where or how to start living out their dreams or passions or what their dreams or passions are, but willing to find out so they can be profiting from their self-employment.

This book is for everyone that was told that they need to stay where it's safe and comfortable and not pursue their desire to work at what they love, because it's not possible to make an income from it.

This book is for those that in-spite of their fears, in-spite of the nay slayers in-spite of how things looks, you are determine to put a plan in action to make your transition from cubical to entrepreneurship less stressful.

I applaud you for being bold enough to go after your dreams and willing to take action to make them happen!

HOW TO USE THIS BOOK

This book is set up with 30 days of **THE SUBJECT** followed by **YOUR ACTION STEP**. The reason I chose this process and kept it simple is so that you will be more motivated and encouraged to take actions and not become overwhelmed.

It's to help you get from where you are to where you want to be by creating a plan you can use to get there. It's not all inclusive, but it gives you a great start. If you start this book with a month that has 31 days on the 31st day I want you to use that day to write out your plan. Bring together all you've been working on for the month by tweaking and re-tweaking as needed to create your one page business plan. If you started this book during the month with 30 days I want you take an extra day and complete the above.

There is a blank page between each page so that you will have enough room to write out your responses to "**Your Action Steps**."

The Suggested Resource Page is of some of the products I've used and are aware that they can help you in your business. Some I'm affiliated member and get paid a commission based on your purchases and others are free. If the links don't work you might have to copy and paste.

Please read the beginning directions at the beginning of the resource page as it provides another value tool you can attain.

DAY 1

THE SUBJECT:

Now that you have decided you need to make a change in your career, but have no clue where you need to begin to start your new journey. Below is where I'll have you start.

When I do a coaching session with a client I have them start with one of the most important questions I learned from my "Outside-the-Job-Box" certification course with Dr. Valerie Young of www.changingcourse.com, **What do I Want My Life to Look Like?** A lot of people ask you what you want to be when you grow up, but they never ask you what you want your life to look like. In answering this question you can take the step to creating the life you want to truly live.

Here are three (3) questions to consider to build your plan of **What do you Want**? I encourage you to write down your answer to these questions and keep them in the forefront of your mind and life throughout the year so as you start looking at making your career transition you can make sure it fit YOUR life test.

- **What time would I like to wake up?** Are you a day person or night owl? Do you know when is **YOUR** most optimal time of the day is? If not figure this out.

- **What do I want to see when I look out my window?** Is it a meadow, the mountain, the ocean, a lake, a garden, the desert, a skyline, a park, the Big Bend, etc.? Do you want to stay where you are now are would you like to move? If you're not able to move at this time then how can you get closer to the goal you want?

- **How would I spend my morning?** Would I exercise, mediate, read, have coffee on your deck, porch, or at a coffee shop, would you like to play a round of golf, get in a game of tennis, go for a swim, or take a nice stroll?

YOUR ACTION STEP:

Answer the three questions above by writing out your answers below so you can view it on a daily basis.

Moving Forward

DAY 2

THE SUBJECT:

You wonder if it's at all possible to make money at what you love. I say a resounding **YES!**

Next you wonder what steps you need to take to make this happen.

My advice to you would be, begin finding out what you truly love doing and if you really want to make money at it or keep it as a hobby?

The following are a few examples of how you can make money at what you love:

- If you love alternative/herbal remedies and writing - Use your writing skills to write about subjects that are interesting to you and input your knowledge concerning alternative/herbal remedies. You'll be able to create information products to sale.

- If you enjoy researching and alternative/herbal remedies - You can set up a membership site that would allow your members to submit a form for you to research the best and least expensive place or places to buy the herbs they are interested in buying. You ask, "Why would anyone pay me to do this?" Because, everyone is busy with life and has little time to do all the research. You're providing them with a service that saves them time and money. Plus, this process would be a personalized plan just for them and their needs.

- What if you love travel and alternative/herbal remedies - You could set up group trips to the best places to buy herbs. You could also include educational information on each herb and what they are good for.

- If you love travel, cooking and alternative/herbal remedies - You could schedule cooking classes on which herbs are good to use in cooking and how to cook with them. You could set up group trips to the various regions where herbs come from set up cooking classes with the local that shows which herbs are good to use in cooking and how to cook with them. This could be done in State or abroad.

YOUR ACTION STEP:

Now is your time!

What are the things that you truly love doing?

Write out how to combine these items and create work that you love.

DAY 3

THE SUBJECT:

Follow your own bent, no matter what people say. ~ Karl Marx

So many people, including and especially those closest to you, will tell you to stay where you are because at least you have a job even though you are miserable. They either love you too much to see you leave the familiar or they are people who are afraid of taking the necessary steps to get out of their own miserable situation.

Don't abandon your hopes and dreams because someone else cannot envision them. Start now while you're sitting at your cubicle putting your dream(s) into place by:

1.   Working on your plans and writing them out

2.   Setting things up for your departure from where you are now to where you are going

3.   Working through your own fears (**look at day 5**)

4.   Doing as much research and paperwork on and for your new career/adventure

5.   Take a class, tele or video course on what you are interested in.

Remember if you follow your own bent, not everyone will agree or support you, but that doesn't mean it is the wrong thing or time to do it.

YOUR ACTION STEP:

Of the 5 suggestions above which do you plan to do tomorrow?

Moving Forward

DAY 4

THE SUBJECT:

Perseverance what a powerful word this is. According to Merriam-Webster dictionary it is the action or fact or an instance of persevering: continued or steadfast pursuit or prosecution of an undertaking or aim. According to Edmund Burke dictionary it is the condition or power of persevering: persistence in the pursuit of objectives or prosecution of any project.

While the 2012 Olympic Games over a two week period the one thing that kept coming to mind was how easy and effortless some of the athletes made it all look, but I realized that it wasn't easy and through all the featured stories of various athletes it was confirmed. What these athletes had to do is **persevere** through a variety of things in their lives in order to reach their goal of being in the Olympics and possible winning gold.

The same happens to those of us who are solo-entrepreneurs as we are building and re-creating our businesses. There are a lot we have to **persevere** through in order to make our businesses successful and appear effortless. Just like the athletes, we all have a back story as to why we wanted to start our own businesses. We know the Olympians do all for the gold, the pride of their country, and personal pride.

YOUR ACTION STEP:

What is the reason for you to **perseverance** to succeed in starting your business? What's your reason to **PUSH FORWARD**?

Moving Forward

DAY 5

THE SUBJECT:

We all deal with fear at some point in both our lives and businesses. This can be more so when you are in the process of making a transition in your career or personal life. The goal is to avoid having your fears turn into anxiety, phobias, and panic attacks. Here are some ways to fight through your fears:

- **Remember you are human and fear is real** - allow yourself to feel your fear recognize it and allow yourself to work through that fear.

- **Meet fear head on and own up to it** – the more you try to hide your fear and put your head in the sand, the more it will keep eating at you and take away your power.

- **Talk about and share it** – I've learned that the more you talk about your fear the less hold it will have over you, and the less hold it has over you the more you will be able to move past it. Have a good CRY it will be worth it in the long run.

- **Ask for help in handling your fears** – from your higher power, trusted family members and friends, your support group (networking group), etc. The more help you have the more you find fear fading.

- **Have a balance in your life** – I know you're asking what does having a balance in your life have to do with handling your fears? I've learned when there is a balance in your life, and fear rears its ugly head you can handle it more effectively by having something else to focus on. Once you no longer focus on the fear and allow yourself the freedom of doing something else you will find you are able to get back to the fear and it doesn't look as scary and you're able to handle it more efficiently and effectively!

Two definition of "FEAR" I came up with for myself:
- Facing Every Amazing Road©
- Finally Experiencing All Riches© (not just monetarily)

YOUR ACTION STEP:

Which step from above will YOU work on to help YOU deal with YOUR fear?

Moving Forward

DAY 6

THE SUBJECT:

Take calculated risks. That is quite different from being rash. ~George S. Patton

This is important to remember as you prepare to make the change from the cubical world to the working at what you love. During this time of fear, concern about the economy, personal strife, etc., it's important that you take the calculated risk and not be rash due to all the things I mentioned earlier.

It's easier said than done, I know, that's why it's important to make a plan and stick with it. Don't fail to plan, because it will help you stay on track! Only you know what's in you and what you're capable of doing. You have to remember that you're cable of doing more than you think that's why it's important to find those who will support you and take the necessary steps towards **YOUR** goal(s) and true joy.

YOUR ACTION STEP:

What calculated risks are you prepared to take to achieve your dreams?

Moving Forward

DAY 7

THE SUBJECT:

Beyond the mountains there are mountains again. ~ Haitian proverb

There will always be something to get in the way of you achieving your goal of working at what you love. You have to remember it won't be extremely easy and if it sounds too good to be true then it probably is.

If you are aware of this then you need to know that it will take a lot of determination, drive, perseverance, a plan that you will stick to, etc. to get to the point of being able to leave your cubicle job and start working at what you love and love what you're doing.

It is possible and attainable, but you have to be willing to continue to work towards your goals to get over those tall mountains that will eventually become smaller so that you can cross over a little easier.

YOUR ACTION STEP:

What mountain is standing in your way of achieving your goal of working at what you love? What is one step you can take to move that mountain?

Moving Forward

DAY 8

THE SUBJECT:

Great things are not done by impulse, but by a series of small things brought together ~Vincent van Gogh

We hear about job losses and layoffs every day and it can be very discouraging, but there is a silver lining.

As I travel and stay in a lot of small towns/cities throughout the country and Canada I see a lot of small/one business owners making it work and helping to keep our country running. I'm reminded how this country was built on small/one business owners (True Entrepreneurs). It's how we got our start and it's what will continue to keep this country going.

Remember that all large businesses had to start somewhere and most started out small. If they can do it so can you. Just start small, keep your ideas and determination fresh and you'll be surprised as to where it leads you!

YOUR ACTION STEP:

What is one idea that you've had in your head, but never put on paper?

Moving Forward

DAY 9

THE SUBJECT:

What would you attempt to do if you knew you would not fail? ~ Robert Schuller

This is an awesome question...have you ever thought about it?

Allow yourself to dream and dream big. Most of us are afraid to even try anything because we are afraid of failing, but it you knew you would not fail what is it you would attempt to do?

It is never too late and at this point in your life you're not too old to consider it. I know personally of a 63-year-old who went back to massage school to become a massage therapist something she has always wanted to do, but could never find the time until she turned 63 and I have other similar stories like this.

Since most of us recognize that we will now have to work longer than originally planned, why not work at what you love and love what you're doing? I know it's scary but, life is too short for regrets!

YOUR ACTION STEP:

Ask yourself – What would you attempt to do if you knew you would not fail?

DAY 10

THE SUBJECT:

To succeed, you need to find something to hold on to, something to motivate you, something to inspire you. ~ Tony Dorsett

We all want to be able to succeed in whatever it is that we do.

We want to be able to enjoy the fruits of our labour. If this is true, what is it that you need to hold on to, because it intrigues you so much and make you want to make it work?

What is it that motivates you enough to make you stick with it even through the rough times?

What it is that inspires you enough to make you want to get out of bed every day with a smile on your face, a song in your heart, a joy in your spirit, a desire to work, and to see it through from start to finish.

Whatever it is, if you have these three things pushing you forward then you will succeed and be working at what you love.

YOUR ACTION STEP:

What motivates, inspires, and intrigues you enough that you can't wait to get out of bed to go do?

Moving Forward

DAY 11

THE SUBJECT:

When Whitney Houston made her come back in 2009 one of the songs on her I Look to You album called - **I Didn't Know My Own Strength**.

As I was listening to and reading the words to this song, I realized that there have been times, even now, that I don't know my own strength. I realized if I don't always know my own strength, then, that means some of you don't know yours either!

Not just in life, but in business also, we are a strong and resilient people!

> **Strong** - able to bear or endure, able to withstand stress or violence: not easily broken or injured, having or exhibiting moral or intellectual force, endurance, or vigor, and effective or efficient especially in a particular direction: able to accomplish a result.

> **Resilient** - to jump back, rebound, capable of withstanding shock without permanent deformation or rupture, moving swiftly back, and tending to regain strength or high spirits after weakness or depression.

Moving Forward

You can accomplish whatever it is you set your mind to if you can just recognize your own strength, and take that all important first step(s) and action(s). Every time I acknowledge, accept, and believe in my own strength I accomplish more than I thought I ever could. God gives us all that we need to move forward to make great and powerful things happen if we just believe and recognize "ALL" that He has put within us!

YOUR ACTION STEP:

As you are making preparation to transition from cubical to entrepreneurship, remember that you **"can"** do what you set your mind to do because, everything you need is in you and you can do anything you want including recreating who you are and what you want to do now that you're starting a new journey!

What have you recognized inside yourself that will help you start your new journey?

DAY 12

THE SUBJECT:

Why do you work part-time jobs? For various reasons including, but not limited to, paying off bills, purchase new stuff (needed and for fun), pay for college, to save, to take a trip, or to have some extra money in our pockets (as my maternal grandmother use to say "some pocket change").

If you're going to work part-time anyways why not think about working to fund your own dreams and passion, too fund your new career versus working just to be working, and in the process create work that you love doing? This will also give you a chance to see if what you think is something you truly want to do is really what you want to do and if not, then you can mark it off your list and move on to the next thing.

If one of the reasons you are hesitant to leave your current position is because of lack of money, I encourage you sit down and do a couple of things:

1. Think about working part-time and what it is you truly would like to do.

2. Allow yourself to honestly think about how much money you will need to set aside to fund your dream.

3. Set up boundaries that will allow you to stick your goal and not stray from those boundaries.

YOUR ACTION STEP:

What is it you truly want to do when you transition from cubical to entrepreneurship and what part-time position are you willing to take on to achieve this dream?

DAY 13

THE SUBJECT:

Let me first say you have to define what **SUCCESS** means for you. Not what others say it is, but what your **SUCCESS** looks like. I know a lot of people have written on this subject and like a lot of you I've had to get a true meaning of what my SUCCESS looks like for me. Once I've done that, I've allowed myself to judge if what goals I set out to achieve this year was a success or not.

Even if you didn't complete all of your goals, that doesn't mean you didn't succeed. The fact that you took the necessary steps to achieve your goals is a success. We beat ourselves up way too much and don't view the small steps we take as a success. I'm here to tell you even the smallest steps is just as important, valuable, and worth just as much as completing the whole task.

Remember there are a lot of people that will never take a step or even try to work at what they love and reach their dreams in life.

YOUR ACTION STEP:

1. What is **YOUR** definition of Success?

2. What is **ONE** small step you plan to take today to get you on your road to success in life and/or business?

DAY 14

THE SUBJECT:

There are a lot of good things to be said for loyalty, but I want you to think about how sometimes loyalty stops you from possible moving forward towards your dreams and passion.

Some of us are loyal to fault and what happens a lot of times is we won't try something new because, we're hesitant to go or do something different and in turn we misses out on new possibilities, go in a different direction, miss an exciting path, because we want to stay with what we know.

Another issue of being loyal to fault is that people and companies don't appreciate or care about our loyalty to them and move to feeling entitled versus being appreciative that we continue to come to them because we believe in what they have to offer. This is one of the reasons I feel customer service has gone out the window.

There is nothing wrong with being loyal, it's when we as the client chooses to use it as an excuse to not move forward and as a business when we feel that sense of entitlement so we treat our customers or clients without respect because we think and feel they **have** to come to us is when it becomes a challenge.

YOUR ACTION STEP:

How do you deal with YOUR own loyalty, do you use it as an excuse not to try something new, take an exciting path or do you use it as a form of entitlement and choose to treat others without respect?

DAY 15

THE SUBJECT:

Learn to Be Grateful. When you find yourself in a grateful place you will find that more things will fall into place in your life. I know we find it hard to be grateful when life and our world seems to be falling apart, but let me tell you, if you can work from a place and space of gratitude it won't seem as bad as you think.

So you ask how do you work from a place and space of gratitude when you are in the process of transiting, losing, or retiring from a career and there is nothing on the horizon, bills are due, food need to be put on the table, doctors need to be visited, and there don't seem to be any light at the end of the tunnel!

I will share with you how I've work from that place of gratitude when all hope seems to be gone.

> First I connect with my spiritual side and allow it to speak to me.
> Secondly, I focus on those things that are right in my life and world and let all other stuff go.
> Thirdly, I don't allow myself to look, read, or be around things or individuals that are negative so it doesn't feed into my being.
> Fourthly, I find positive individuals that will support me through the down time.
> Fifthly, I acknowledge and allow myself my mourning moments, but I don't wallow there for too long.
> Last, but not least, I believe with all that is in me and visualize that it will and has gotten better (notice I said **has** not **have**, keeping it in the present tense). I keep moving forward until I'm at that place of gratitude and I realize that nothing can stop me unless I let it!

YOUR ACTION STEP:

From the list above what is **one** thing that you can do to start going or staying in your place of gratitude? If something else comes to mind that is not on the list don't hesitate to write it down. This is to help you and my list is not a catch all list!

Moving Forward

DAY 16

THE SUBJECT:

Words have Power and the words that you choose to use can play a role in what and how you choose to take the next step in going from cubicle to entrepreneurship. One of my mentors and business coach told me to be aware of the words I use as I move forward in growing my business.

When fighting a life alternating illness, I learn how powerful words really were as I was focusing on healing. When I decided to go from cubicle to entrepreneurship, I realized that my words along with action can and has influenced my work.

I've put some powerful and positive words in front of me and I keep them there so when I find myself hitting my wall, I can regroup and refocus where I'm going not where I am now.

As you are in preparation of MOVING FORWARD and stepping into the next phase of your life; I want you to be conscious of the words you allow to cross your eyes and set up shop in your mind.

Create your own journal of positive words, phrases, scriptures, quotes, etc. that will help you prepare for your journey. Put them where you can see and read them every day especially when you or someone one else speak negatively about your dreams.

You will be able to power through the negativity if you allow yourself to counter it with positive. I know it may sounds a little "whoo whoo" to some of you, but trust me it truly works!

YOUR ACTION STEP:

Come up with five positive words, phrases, scriptures, or quotes, you can start reading and saying for the next 30 days that will keep you focus on your dreams and goals so when you begin your journey of transiting into entrepreneurship you will be a ready and able to handle where you are going!

DAY 17

THE SUBJECT:

I saw this ad online with a young woman looking happy and satisfied and at the end of the ad it said, "find your own version of happiness now!" It was an online dating service ad, but the slogan really stuck with me.

Find your own version of happiness not only applies to the "personals", but this philosophy can be applied and will work in finding the right career as well.

All you need to do is to get into the right mind-set, sit down and document on paper/computer what happiness looks like to you and this helps you to understand what direction you take to make your happiness a reality.

Arm yourself with the necessary tools to get you from point A to point B, add drive and a strong belief that you can and will do it, and then take action to make it happen.

Your version of happiness doesn't have to be mainstream or traditional; it needs to be **your** very own personal version of what will make you happy. Set out today on **your** own personal path, have fun in finding **your** own version of happiness and remember what the great Arthur Ashe said, "Success is a journey, not a destination. The doing is often much more important than the outcome."

YOUR ACTION STEP:

Sit down write out what will make you truly happy and what that happiness looks like.

DAY 18

THE SUBJECT:

I encourage you to take on the mindset of stopping "biting off more than you can chew." Meaning stop overextending yourself! When you find out that you have overextended yourself take a step back look at what you have on your plate that's allowing you from moving forward.

Overextending can bring on anxiety, procrastination, lack of energy, lack of excitement for what you're doing, and lack of focus. It shouldn't be hard to let go, but sometimes that happens, because we feel guilty if we find ourselves in the position of possible letting someone down or not completing the task we started to begin with.

A few steps that I would suggest you put in place to attempt overextending yourself are the following:

1. Does what you are about to take on feed your dreams?

2. Why is it you want to do what it is you're thinking about doing and how will it fit into your current schedule?

3. What is the "true/realistic" time versus the "appearance of" time will it take for you to do the extra task.

As you deal with this I want you to remember not to make it hard on others that need to let go! Be respectful of their decision to move on and forward. Just remember how you felt when someone kept you where you found yourself staying because you didn't feel comfortable of letting them down.

YOUR ACTION STEP:

When you've found yourself in an overextended positions, how did you get there?

What do you tell yourself when you've committed to doing whatever?

Did you have a clear plan of what it was going to take to do the task?

After answering the questions above, I want you do an assessment of how you can do better and what guardrails you can put in place to help you from continuing overextending yourself?

DAY 19

THE SUBJECT:

When thinking about retiring we think about all we will do and get accomplished once we don't have to clock in and answer to anyone else again. What we forget about is that once we retire we still have to take some action.

We dream about how we don't have to get up to a clock, but what we don't do is plan on what we're going to do once we **do** get up. We also tend to forget about all the things that still need to be taken care of financially.

We forget, as a friend of mine made me aware of, that $1500 extra to our existing pay check is different from $1500 that we have to live off of for a full month. Think about that for a minute!

Some of us don't plan our retirement, but just talk about it. Not only do we just talk about it, we take **no** action. We have a plan without considering the actions we have to take to reach our goal.

Here are a few things to consider as you are planning to retire or leave your job:

1. Do you even have an idea of what you truly want to do?
2. Have you researched your idea and found out if it's truly what you want to do or is it just an idea in your head?
3. Do you have a plan in place and with that plan do you have what action or actions are required to bring that plan to fruition?
4. Do you know what you want your life to look like once you're retired or start your new business venture?
5. If you decide that you don't want to do anything, do you have enough to get you through? Not only

Moving Forward

financially, but mentally, socially, and creatively to get you through the doing nothing time? Because you still need to feed your mind, body, and soul even when you're retired. If you don't then you find yourself just withering away.

YOUR ACTION STEP:

There is only so much of "nothing" you can do once you retire. You need to address this issue as well as the financial piece. As you can see, there is a lot more to retirement than just financially preparing. Have you really prepared to retire?

DAY 20

THE SUBJECT:

When life gets in the way and I have a lot on my heart and mind, I have to step back and take a much needed break!

It reminds me of one of the many reasons I wanted to be an entrepreneur. I am able to step back when I need to without having to ask someone for permission. When I need to take time off, don't have to worry if I have enough vacation days. I am free to go to the one place that allows me to regroup and come back renewed which is my quilting.

Quilting is one of the ways I renew, revive, re-adjust, regroup, relax, think, clear my mind, heart, and spirit, and last but not least I get to create, which is something I truly enjoy.

It's important as solo-entrepreneurs we have that special thing we do or place that we need to go to in order take a much needed mental break! Our business and clients need for us to work at our optimum levels.

YOUR ACTION STEP:

Do you have something that takes you to that level when you've hit your wall and need to regroup in order to take action towards working at what you love? If so what is it? If not think about what you want it to be (if could be personal). If you don't have an answer to either, then what would you like it to be?

DAY 21

THE SUBJECT:

Sitting here going through my end of year evaluation for my life, I'm making the necessary changes to my business model by writing out my life plan for the upcoming year.

I realized that the past year didn't end the way I wanted, but I choose to celebrate those things that went right! Then find new and creative ways to make those things that didn't go the way I planned go better for this year.

Below are a few suggestions I have for you to make your life plan go better:

– **Break your plans and systems down to manageable tasks** that way you will get them completed and not just have them sitting in your head and this will also help with the procrastination.

– **Focus on those things that are working right** in your life instead of focusing on what is wrong. Once your mindset is thinking on the good then working on those things that you want to improve will not seem so bad or difficult to achieve!

– Choose to **surround yourself with those that will honestly support your vision** and help to hold you accountable for the things that you want to put into place in a supportive, but determined way.

– **Speak to yourself and think about your life in a kind and successful way!** Our mindset and words plays an important role in your lives and your success. Don't allow yourself to speak to YOU in a way that you would not allow others to speak to you. Know that you are worth every bit of success that you set for yourself and your life!

YOUR ACTION STEP:

For each step above what is one thing you plan to do to take the step towards putting it together for yourself?

Moving Forward

DAY 22

THE SUBJECT:

As I was looking behind, beneath, and between the cushions of my couch for something that I had misplaced, I found several other items I had been searching for quite some time now. Why is it when we are looking for one thing we find something else? Not only did I find the something I'd been looking for, but I also found a lot of dirt, dust and other things that had fallen under and behind the couch. So I cleaned up the area, picked up the items and moved on.

This got me to thinking, we need to set aside time to look behind and under our personal couches that can help encourage versus to take action towards becoming an entrepreneur. There's no telling what golden nuggets we might find and what "stuff" we need to clean up, delete, stop receiving, and/or re-visit.

I realized I have some very useful items that I've moved to my "save" folder in my email box and I've never looked at them again. Instead of buying another item, tele-seminar, and/or program, or signing up for another "free" tele-class, tele-seminar, and receive another free report; I'm making the commitment to myself to go through my "save" messages and schedule time to read through, listen to, and get through each one at a time until the folder is empty.

YOUR ACTION STEP:

What is ONE item that you have saved in email or on your computer that you can listen to, read, take a look at and then take action?

Moving Forward

DAY 23

THE SUBJECT:

I was watching Serena Williams in her 2010 semi-final Australian Open game against a challenging Chinese player Na Li, it hit me how hard Serena had to fight in this match. Even though she was not having her best game, she was taped up, worn, looking a little tired, and having to fight hard without help on the court, but she kept fighting. She literally fought her way through that match and on the other end was a win and a spot to play for it all in the finals.

But before she could go rest and recoup from her singles match she had to go play the semi-final doubles with her sister Venus. I'm sure she had to dig deep within herself to refocus, be ready to play, put herself back in that competitive mode and hit the court with her sister to play their game and to play to win.

You ask what does this have to do with you and becoming an entrepreneur. Sometimes we're going to find ourselves in our businesses having to fight to keep it all going even when we feel like giving up, when we're tired and wounded, when we don't have the support or finances, or when we can't see the end of the tunnel. Life will throw our businesses in a tail spin and we find ourselves in our singles match on court without any help or coaching and we have to fight hard through the game in order to win.

Yes, our supporters, fans, coaches, and networking groups are in the stands cheering us on, but they cannot play the game for us (run our business for us). In the end it is our responsibility to make it work and make it a success. **AND** like Serena, we find that after we've won our match, before we can rest and recoup there's something else waiting for us to do. It's easy to give up, but to succeed we're going to have to be willing to keep going, dig deep for our courage, pull our head out of the sand, and get back to work. Are you willing to fight today and every day for your business to succeed?

By the way Serena and Venus won their semi-final doubles match later and went on to play in the finals.

YOUR ACTION STEP:

When you find your back against the wall and too tired to keep going, what is it that you plan to do to keep focus and keep going?

DAY 24

THE SUBJECT:

Have you ever done something yourself because paying someone to do what you believe you can learn just doesn't make sense to you? I challenge you to think about what it's costing you every time you are taken away from your income producing items to learn these new techniques?

If you've never thought about this let me give you an example - If you provide coaching services and you charge $200 an hour and you take 3 hours out of your schedule to work on your bookkeeping, when you could have hired a bookkeeper to do this for you at $10-$20 an hour, then you just cost yourself $600 when you could have spent $30-$60 instead!

I find myself technically challenged, however, when my website went down I decided that I would try to figure out the problem since my web person was on vacation. This truly cost me a lot of time and money, not to mention some peace of mind. Because, I spent too much time trying to get back online when it probably would have taken my web person a few minutes to do the task.

What I found out in the process is:

- By not understanding the language and having the lack of knowledge and understanding I was getting only pieces of the problem solved instead of getting everything I needed at once.
- I took steps that I didn't need to take, because I was not totally understanding what was and was not required.
- It's not a good idea to be the in-between person. By talking to my web designer via email and text messages and trying to relay that information to the

technical customer service personnel this caused more and more frustration and time!

- Need to make sure to have a back-up plan and it will be worth the extra cost not to have to deal with situations that allow me to end up totally frustrated, almost in tears, feeling lost and useless, and being unproductive which resulted in loss of income!

YOUR ACTION STEP:

Figure out What Your Time Worth?

Moving Forward

DAY 25

THE SUBJECT:

How important is it to have systems in place for your business? One of my mentors, and business coach, Allison Phillips spoke about putting systems in place to help you navigate through your business. Once you apply the technique of putting systems in place for everything you do in your business, you will find that you can apply it to other areas of your life.

I remember when I was in the military we had check-lists/systems/policies and procedures (our regulations) in order to run every aspect of our jobs and offices smoothly and to allow anyone that might come in to take your place the ability to just step in and run our projects without having a work stoppage. So, if it worked and continues to work for the military why not apply the same concept to your business.

If you write the system(s) down, which I highly advise, this will allow you to create an information product(s)!

YOUR ACTION STEP:

What is one system that you can put into place to help you run your business or life more efficiently?

Moving Forward

DAY 26

THE SUBJECT:

As long as one keeps searching, the answers come. ~ Joan Baez

Are you always searching for answers and getting frustrated with not finding the answer you have been looking for? Understand you are not alone. I've found myself in this position a time or two, but what I've learned is that as long as we keep searching the answers do eventually come. In fact, much of the time we already have the answers, we just don't know it and we can also find other hidden gems that will allow us to move forward in our decision to create a life and work that we love.

4 things I've learned through consistent searching:

✓ I am stronger than I ever thought and that strength allows me to accomplish whatever I put my mind to.

✓ I have everything I need to make my business the success I want it to be.

✓ What is mine no one can take from me unless I choose to give it up!

✓ To take a folder and title it "Learning File", because not ALL of the lessons that I've learned during my search quest was for right then, but for a future date! When I need that lesson then all I had to do is pull out my folder to view at the appropriate time.

YOUR ACTION STEP:

Take a step back, take a deep breath, relax, and truly listen to what is going on around you and you just might find you can hear your answers.

DAY 27

THE SUBJECT:

When doing an embroidery quilt, I can set my sewing machine and leave it to do its thing! BUT every now and then I find I've left my machine, to do something else while it's embroidering, and when I get back I find a thread might have broken, it missed some stitches, and/or it's ready for me to change thread colors or designs.

In your business you'll want to set it and leave it, but if you're not minding what's yours something could go wrong or require your attention. Because you've set it and left it you could find yourself in a difficult or unplanned situation at some time or another. Even with an auto pilot business, your business still requires your attention even if you leave it in the hands of others that you trust. Sometimes I have to monitor my sewing machine to asses what's going on and why something's not working properly.

It's important you be present in your business even with an auto pilot type of business. Because, you need to be aware of what's going on to avoid the big or unexpected surprises!

YOUR ACTION STEP:

What action plan will you put in place to avoid the big or unexpected surprises that can occur in business?

DAY 28

THE SUBJECT:

When quilting I find I have to make some adjustments to what I'm working on for various reasons. In business, there are going to be times that you'll have to make adjustments due to things not fitting what you're doing any longer, something went wrong with your project, someone didn't show up for a meeting or a speaker got ill and can't make it.

It's so easy for us to get wigged out instead of thinking about how to either change what we've done or have a contingency plan in place. Life happens. Things happen and we have to learn to adjust when they do and create a better process to handle.

I have to admit I don't always handle adjustments on the fly well. I'm one that has to take a step back, think about it, and look at it from different angles before I make a decision. Which means I'm the one that has to have a contingency plan in place to help me avoid the big "freak out."

YOUR ACTION STEP:

Write down what you plan to do when you have to make adjustments in your business and how you would like to handle that process when you do.

DAY 29

THE SUBJECT:

I went to a meeting for a particular product and I went to buy! At this meeting they went over the various products and then proceeded to the business plan, but they made it very clear that the products are for everyone, while the business plan is not. So once the meeting was over I wanted to find out how much it would cost me to get the items I wanted.

Instead of giving me the price, the person kept talking about the products, what they do, and the scientific facts of it all and about the business plan. Once again, I asked about the cost of the products I was interested in, because I already knew what I wanted to buy.

Instead of them listening to what I was saying they kept going on about everything except what I was interested in. It grated my nerves so bad that I couldn't wait to get out of the place and I realize now I have to find someone else who sells this product line to get the items I want.

The sad part is they don't realize that they lost a valuable client. Because, they were so busy trying to sell me on stuff I wasn't interested in and neglected to understand what my needs and desires were.

Know your clients! Listen, and I mean **truly** listen to them. Most will let you know what their needs, wants, and desires are. There are very few that have to be pushed into getting what they really want and if they do, then they are probably not your ideal client.

Once a client makes up their mind what it is they want, most are ready to purchase without any additional prodding or pushing. Sometimes we are so focused on giving the person more than what they need or have asked for that we miss out on the sale and a repeat buyer. Sometimes the more info you give the more you talk yourself right out of a sale!

YOUR ACTION STEP:

What will you do to make sure you won't talk your clients out of _____ (fill in the blank)?

Moving Forward

DAY 30

THE SUBJECT:

When you make the decision to transition from cubicle to entrepreneurship and start your business you'll find individuals approaching you to consider partnering with them, doing collaboration or join them in joint venture. You find yourself not truly understanding what they mean or how they can best help you in your business or how you can best help them in theirs.

After completing some research to understand the difference between the three so that when another person ask me to do either I would know which was a better fit for me or if it was worth doing.

The following are the definition according to Wikipedia:

Collaboration – is when two or more people or organizations work together to realize a shared goals.

Joint Venture – is a business agreement in which parties agree to develop, for a finite time and a specific project. It's when two or more persons come together to form a temporary partnership for the purpose of carrying out a particular project.

Partnership – is a legal arrangement where parties agree to cooperate to advance their mutual interests. It is formed between one or more business in which partners (owners) co-labor to achieve and share profits and losses.

Even though these terms have been used interchangeable, the two that are the closes are Collaboration and Joint Venture. Since Partnership is a legal agreement you will find yourself not using this form of entity unless you've set your business up this way.

Moving Forward

As a self-employed/solo-entrepreneur you will be collaborating or entering into a joint venture with another person. Because when we are in business for ourselves we are not in business by ourselves! You will find yourself needing to collaborate with others to reach a shared goal, i.e. help increase your client list by sharing it, or entering into a joint venture to host a workshop by bringing both your strong points to create a more powerful workshop.

YOUR ACTION STEP:

List at least 3 people you would like to work with and in what capacity?

Day 31:

One Page Business Plan

Use this day to write out your One Page Business Plan from all the information that you've written out over the past 30 days. Bring it all together in an orderly fashion for you.

SUGGESTED RESOURCES

At the time of print all links are correct and working. If you're not able to click on the links or they don't work, try copying and pasting. If the link is broken don't hesitate to contact me at karen@giveyourselfpower.com for additional help.

If you purchased the paperback book and would like to receive the links via email or you're interested in receiving any new or updated resources once a month for up to 90 days after your purchase. Click on the following link and write in the comment section "Add me to the 90 day new and updated resource list." http://www.giveyourselfpower.com/contact

Domain Name and Hosting:

- Host Gator - http://secure.hostgator.com/~affiliat/cgi-bin/affiliates/clickthru.cgi?id=GivePower

- Blue Host - http://www.bluehost.com/track/givepower

- 1and1 - http://www.1and1.com/?k_id=156307995

- How to Get More Clients Instant Access to 11 Free Videos - http://www.autowebbusiness.com/app/?Clk=4251392

- Need to Raise Money - https://www.e-junkie.com/ecom/gb.php?cl=251652&c=ib&aff=133659

- Get Paid for Referrals - http://tinyurl.com/lgy76mv

- Get Paid to Brainstorm - https://changingcourse.infusionsoft.com/go/cc/a215
- To build an online business - http://www.nicheology.com/index.cfm?affID=KarenHeck

- Piggy Back Product Launches: Cool Little Tactics to Leverage High-Impact Influential Partners - http://www.nicheology.com/public/397.cfm?affID=KarenHeck

- Want to Create a Membership Site - http://ac7oc8stpjqisg7-kjoeuh8b18.hop.clickbank.net/?tid=WISHLIST

- Ready2Go Marketing – http://www.1shoppingcart.com/app/?Clk=5094286

- Become a Confident Tele-seminar Leader - http://www.1shoppingcart.com/app/?af=1483871

- Free 52 Week Email Program - http://www.1shoppingcart.com/app/?Clk=4850980

- Free Conference Call – https://www.freeconferencecall.com

- Manage Your Social Media Accounts for Free – https://hootsuite.com/
- You can sign up for a Free 30 day Trial of Hootsuite Pro - http://www.kqzyfj.com/dq122mu2-u1HPKKLLLOHJIRQOLJI

- Free Autoresponder and Newsletter Program – http://eepurl.com/DnWfX

- Need motivation and connect to a local networking group for less than $10 a month with the iLiving App – http://www.iLivingApp.com/karenheck/

- Want to get paid for the games, products, and/or services that you refer to others - http://tinyurl.com/lgy76mv

ABOUT THE AUTHOR

Karen Washington-Heck is a founder of Give Yourself Power, LLC. She created her business to help other achieve their goal of leaving their "job-job" and enter into the wonderful world of entrepreneurship. Karen is truly passionate about solo-entrepreneurs and work-from-home individuals and want to help more and more people break out of the cubical world and into working at what they love.

Karen comes from a long line of entrepreneurs and understand that entrepreneurs are the back bone of this country. Without millions of people determine to create their own businesses then where would we all be?

Karen is a retired disabled veterans from the United States Air Force. Outside of being an author, she's a motivational speaker with a zing for comedy and reality. She tells it like it is and is open and transparent. She's passionate about helping and encouraging others to go after what they want in life. She's the best cheerleader you could have on your team due to her supportive spirit.

She loves to travel, read, write and spend time with her loving and supportive husband, Richard Heck. She's been in business for herself off and on most of her adult life, because, in her own words, "I love the power and flexibility that entrepreneurship provides me."

Karen would love to hear from you and if you would like to work with her or have her speak at your next event, contact me by going to www.giveyourselfpower.com/contact and or emailing her at karen@giveyourselfpower.com.

Whatever it is you are passionate about let that motivate you to follow your dreams!